DISCLAIMER: This is an UN original book.

It designed to record all the key points of the original book.

It helps you get an overview before or after reading the original book.

If you haven't owned the original book, you can buy it here:

https://www.amazon.com/dp/163565243X

This book is not authorized, approved, licensed, or endorsed by the subject book's author or publisher. **Keynotes** is not associated with the original author in any way.

All rights reserved. No part of this book may be reproduced, duplicated, or spread in any form or by any means without prior written permission of the author or the publisher. This includes uploading, photocopying, scanning, recording, etc. by any digital or other systems.

TABLE OF CONTENTS

Introduction 3
Part I: The Circadian Clock 11
    Chapter 1: All of Us Work Shifts 11
    Chapter 2: The Way Circadian Rhythms Work and the Importance of Timing 20
    Chapter 3: Monitor and Test Whether Your Circadian Code is Synchronized 27
Part II: The Circadian Lifestyle 36
    Chapter 4: A Circadian Code to Optimize Sleep 36
    Chapter 5: Time-restricted Eating: Preparing Your Clock for Weight Loss 47
    Chapter 6: The Best Way to Learn and Work 60
    Chapter 7: Align Your Exercise with your Circadian Code 64
    Chapter 8: Handling the Core Causes of "Disruption": Screens and Light 67
Part III: How to Enhance Circadian Health 71
    Chapter 9: The Clock, Digestive Issues and the Microbiome 71
    Chapter 10: The Circadian Code Helps with Metabolic Syndrome : Heart Disease, Obesity and Diabetes 73
    Chapter 11: To Boost the Immune System and Treat Cancer 75
    Chapter 12: The Circadian Code for Improving Brain Health 76
    Chapter 13: The Best Kind of Circadian Day 77
Conclusion 78
Check out other summaries 79

Introduction

The past century witnessed a substantial change related to human health thanks to germ theory and its associated developments including vaccination, antibiotics, etc. However, even though the human life span has increased in recent times, it does not mean that everyone's health is better. Chronic diseases of the mind and body since an early age have become increasingly common. The cause behind this is today's lifestyle, which contradicts an inherent and cosmic code of health.

The science of circadian rhythms is multidimensional. The author, in collaboration with several others in diverse fields, has discovered that we can restore our rhythm by modifying the timing of the way we live and altering our lifestyles simply. This will mark a revolution in healthcare.

The 'circadian code' entails introducing tiny changes to our manner of eating, sleeping, working, exercising and learning. It will improve our health and home. It is better than medicine or a distinctive diet. Circadian rhythms refer to those biological processes that humans, animals and plants experience as they go about their day. These rhythms are interlinked among species. Further, what controls these rhythms is internal circadian/biological clocks. All cells in our body contain such a clock. All of them are set to turn on or off several thousand genes at different moments during the 24-hour period.

These genes leave an effect on our health in all areas. Good health enables us to sleep better. When we wake up in the morning after sleeping properly, we feel fresh, active and ready for work. Our gut function also works well. Moreover, our hunger works properly and our mind is clear. We have the strength to exercise. When night falls, we are sufficiently exhausted to return to sleep easily.

However, when these rhythms get disturbed for even a single day, our clocks will fail to send the correct signals to these genes, which will cause our mind and body to fail to work properly. If this disturbance persists for some days, weeks or months, we will start experiencing a diverse array of diseases and infections. These might include attention deficit hyperactivity disorder (ADHD), anxiety, depression, insomnia, migraine, obesity, diabetes, cancer, dementia and cardiovascular illnesses.

We can restore such rhythms easily. Our clocks can reach their optimal function in some weeks. Reinstating our circadian rhythms can help us reverse some diseases or speed up their cure.

Biology of Time

The author remembers his childhood in India. He lived in a city with his parents but was amazed by the timely precision with which life unfolded in his paternal grandparents' house in a village. It seemed perfectly synchronized with nature. When the author was in junior high school, his father passed away in a road accident. The author believes that the truck driver that caused the accident must have been sleep-deprived. The author learned later that a sleep-deprived brain is worse than the one influenced by alcohol.

The author also went to an agriculture school after high school like his father. Every living being links to daily and seasonal time. The author noted the differences in the lives of his paternal and maternal grandfathers. While his paternal grandfather lived a rural life perfectly in tune with nature, rising with sunrise and resting with sunset, his maternal grandfather lived an opposite kind of life. The latter served as a goods clerk at a train station and worked the night shift quite often. He experienced dementia in his old age and passed away at the age of 72.

The author's major in college was plant breeding and genetics and he did well. However, he did his master's in molecular biology. This helped the author come face to face with the genetic code. He later secured a research job. During this job, he observed the negative effects of sleep deficiency on worker health. He went to graduate school in Winnipeg, Manitoba, Canada. The shock of temperature change from hot India to cold Canada, long nights and a lack of light left the author feeling blue. When he shifted to San Diego, he dedicated all his focus and attention to the study and research of circadian rhythms. The author has been conducting research in this field for the past 21 years.

The author studied how plants calculate time at the Scripps Research Institute in La Jolla, California as a graduate student. He found out that clock genes exist in both animals and plants. In 2001, he started his postdoctoral research at the Genomic Institute of the Novartis Research Foundation (GNF), where he focused on animal clocks. This institute primarily worked on the human and mouse genome to comprehend biology. The author had a chance to explicate how our circadian rhythms adapt to various seasons or various light categories. A blue light sensor in the eye's retina sends light signals to the brain clock to indicate morning and night. The author is still studying how light affects circadian rhythm and what role modern lighting plays in this procedure.

A breakthrough in research underlined that between hundreds and thousands of genes in the brain and liver switch on and off at particular moments. The author and others are conducting experiments on other parts of the body. The author further launched his own lab at the Salk Institute for Biological Studies and carried on his clock research along with his colleagues.

According to research, having foreseeable and consistent circadian rhythms equals having healthy organs. A genetic code mutation can give rise to illnesses. Similarly, contradicting the circadian code can also bring us closure to illness. The author and cardiovascular and metabolic experts have discovered that the animals that do not have a regular clock are prone to such diseases. A disturbed clock is the root of every single issue. In addition, in a majority of chronic diseases, clock function loses its ability to work properly.

In 2009, light and time, which were the two fields of the author's research, became tangled. In an experiment on mice, researchers found out that each liver gene that switches on and off during a 24-hour span did not take the light signal into account and became synchronized to the time at which the mice had food and fasted. The experiment also showed that a daily eating - fasting cycle steers each liver rhythm. All timing awareness does not stem from the eye's blue light sensor. The earliest morning light resets our brain clock and the earliest morning bite restarts every other organ's clock.

Several studies have demonstrated that when mice have free access to foods full of sugar and fat, they experience obesity and diabetes within a few weeks. In 2012, the researchers conducted an experiment in which they compared a group of mice with free access to the fatty diet to another group that had an 8- to 12-hour span to consume their food. The results were amazing. Mice that consumed the same number of calories from the same foods were fully shielded from diabetes, obesity, heart and liver disease. Sick mice benefitted from this routine without any alteration in their diet or need for medicine.

Other studies on humans have also proved that it's not just the type and quantity of food we eat that matters, it's the timing too. The American Heart Association, the American Diabetes Association and the National Institutes of Health also believe that to protect from or speed up the cure to chronic disease, resetting the circadian clock is the best alternative. The American Heart Association released their first ever meal timing and frequency recommendation in seven decades.

In an environment where approximately one - third of all adults experience at least one chronic disease, including diabetes, obesity, respiratory disease, hypertension, cardiovascular disease, chronic inflammation or asthma, this book presents basic lifestyle changes in the form of simple practices. The book mainly focuses on prevention but we can also use it to improve our lives. Part I of the book helps us recognize the way our circadian clocks work and the reason why sustaining perfect timing is essential for both adults and children. Part II shares guidelines on how to spend our day to optimize our interior rhythms. It will tell us the timing and type of food to eat, but not the quantity.

Part I: The Circadian Clock

Chapter 1: All of Us Work Shifts

All of us are or have functioned as shift workers at some point in time, whether it entails working a night shift, pulling an all-nighter before an exam, managing a baby during nighttime, etc. Partying late for one night can be equally disturbing. Research shows that a huge number of people sleep after midnight or wake up after inadequate sleep. People follow different sleeping schedules during weekdays and weekends. Pregnant women and those with little babies also follow primarily irregular sleep schedules. Working mothers face the biggest challenge in finding a daily rhythm since their schedule is connected to everyone else's at home.

If we cannot sleep properly even one night, we can feel its side effects the next day. Our mind will feel sleep-deprived but we will not be able to sleep. It will negatively affect our muscles and stomach. There will be a constant struggle in our mind since we will want to make up for lost sleep but we will also feel like not sleeping at the same time since it is daytime.

When the brain is working shifts like that, it loses its ability to make rational decisions. Research indicates that one night shift can lead to the kind of cognitive impact that might last an entire week. These memory or attention gaps may cause us to be more prone to bad habits. If we take less sleep for a few days, it might alter our appetite. We might end up consuming junk food at a late hour when our stomach should be resting.

This shift-work mode can cause us to experience challenges in getting to sleep. When some of us take solace in sleeping pills or alcohol, it can lead to depression. Also, addiction to these two solutions can trigger bad habits. It might disturb the sleeping schedules of our family members as well when they try to align their sleep patterns with ours. According to research, children of shift workers are more likely to experience cognitive and behavioral issues than those of non - shift workers. They experience obesity in higher numbers as well.

If we keep disturbing our circadian clock reiteratively, it can negatively affect our health since all our body systems start malfunctioning. It deteriorates our immune system in such a way that germs start attacking us to disturb our stomach. It can even give rise to flulike symptoms. Research indicates that shift workers go through more health issues than non - shift workers. These issues mostly include obesity, diabetes, gastrointestinal problems and cardiovascular problems. Firefighters mostly die or suffer disability because of heart disease. The likely cause is circadian rhythm disturbance. Shift work falls officially into the category of possible carcinogens.

Each one of us will face issues if we are all shift workers. This is why we need to comprehend the way our circadian clocks function so that we can modify our lifestyle to support our body's innate rhythm.

Which Shift Worker Category Do You Belong To?

According to the European definition, a shift worker is a person who sleeps for four or less hours between 10 p. m. and 5 a. m. for more than 50 days in a year. However, the author believes that each one of us is a shift worker because of our lifestyles. The following categories will help you figure out which category you belong to.

Conventional Shift work

Approximately 20 to 25% of the nonmilitary personnel in any country engage in shift work. These include health workers, policemen, emergency responders, air and ground transportation employees, utility service workers, construction and manufacturing workforce, custodial workers, food service workers and call center customer support employees.

Lifestyle Resembling Shift Work

These include performing artists, musicians, high school and college students, mothers of newborns, home caregivers and life partners of shift workers.

Gig Economy Workers

These include freelancers, flexible workers and part-time food delivery service riders and ride - share service drivers.

Jet Lag

This includes traveling between two or more time zones within a 24-hour period.

Social Jet Lag

This refers to the act of a person sleeping late and waking up two or more hours later on the weekend. More than half of the people face this today.

Digital Jet Lag

This refers to the act of chatting with someone who is many time zones away. This will involve staying up for more than 3 hours between 10 p. m. and 5 a. m.

Seasonal Circadian Disturbance

A huge number of people residing in extreme north and south latitudes face more than 16 hours of daylight during summer and less than 8 hours of daylight in winter. This also disturbs the circadian rhythm.

Circadian Rhythms Do Exist

Our timing is not just directed by exterior factors. Internal clocks are real. This is true for plants, animals and humans. An experiment indicated that the circadian rhythm is not precisely 24 hours since in most parts of the universe, the gap between consecutive sunrises is not 24 hours precisely. Our internal clocks adjust to the change in sunrise timing slightly by waking up later or earlier. Circadian rhythms have a link with light.

Daily Life Rhythm

Proper sleep prepares us for the hard work of the next day. A lack of proper sleep will stop us from working properly and sufficiently. A good day's work gets us ready to feel tired and go back to sleep at night without any trouble. The brain generates many hormones at night. These include the sleep hormone melatonin. When we sleep, our brain also generates the human growth hormone. Insufficient sleep equals decreased production of the growth hormone. In children, a lack of sleep can hinder growth. Our brain also detoxifies during sleep.

The Need for Powerful Circadian Rhythms

Circadian rhythms improve biological functions. Each function has its own timing since the body cannot do everything simultaneously. The circadian clocks of newborns are not very functional. This is why they wake up anytime during the night to pass stool or feed. When their circadian rhythm becomes stronger around 5 to 8 months, they are able to regulate their body functions better.

When babies turn into toddlers, their family's timing links with different activities and there is a time for everything. Recognition of light made it possible for our ancestors to wake up at dawn regardless of the season. Our interior timing system is known as the circadian clock. It communicates with light and food timing to give rise to our daily rhythm. We need to sustain this clock for prime health. Therefore, we should synchronize our life with the circadian clock.

Light Confusion

We find it a challenge to live properly in these modern times because insufficient natural light access during the day and excessive bright light exposure during the evening mess up our circadian rhythm. Whether we perform actual shift work or just have a shift - work like lifestyle, circadian disturbance stems from the continuous presence of light at night. It prevents sleep and gives rise to hunger.

Light for Sight and Light for Health are Different

We need to use light properly to improve our health. Bright light and screens at night end up disturbing our circadian rhythms, lessening the sleep hormone melatonin and keeping us up late. It causes insomnia, which leads to anxiety, migraine, annoyance, etc. Therefore, contemporary living makes us prone to several brain illnesses.

With changes in seasons and day length, our circadian rhythms adapt to the alterations in the timings of sunset and sunrise. There is a light-sensing protein in our eyes. It functions as the light sensor that entrains the daily sleep - wake cycle to light. The protein is known as melanopsin. When melanopsin is triggered by recording blue light, it indicates the presence of light to the brain. The brain answers by thinking that it is daytime, no matter what time it actually is. A considerable amount of light is required to activate melanopsin.

Our lifestyle in today's time is such that we spend a substantial amount of time watching bright light indoors and switching bright lights on at night. This triggers melanopsin at indirect moments during daytime and nighttime. This disturbs our circadian rhythms and lessens sleep hormone (melatonin) generation. It further stops us from getting recuperative sleep. The next day after waking up, a lot of our day is spent indoors. The indoor light is not sufficient to initiate melanopsin, which sheds light on our inability to synchronize our circadian clock to the 'day - night' cycle. This causes us to feel sleepy and reduces our alertness. When it keeps happening over a period of time, it gives rise to anxiety and depression.

Therefore, we can introduce small changes in our eye glasses, computer screens and light bulbs to enhance our health.

Chapter 2: The Way Circadian Rhythms Work and the Importance of Timing

Every single living creature experiences the daily anticipated change of the day turning into the night regardless of where they live. Every single living being has created a circadian clock or interior timing system to deal with this predictable daily change.

Every mortal performs some tasks during the 24-hour period. These include getting food (energy), optimizing the utilization of energy by using some of it for daily functioning and storing the remaining amount for using it later, shielding itself from potentially hurtful beasts and agents, mending itself or developing and reproducing. A circadian clock directs all these functions. The clock maximizes every organism's capability to perform these tasks by allocating every single one of these fundamental parts of existence to an ideal time during the day or night. Light does affect circadian rhythms but their timing is regulated by genes internally.

Circadian Clock and Genetics

Our organ health and predisposition to a specific disease depend on the genes we have and the manner of their expression. This refers to whether a particular gene is on or off or if it is a regular or mutant gene. We can gain a considerable amount of knowledge about how genes function and what stems from an anomaly by comparing normal and mutant genes.

The period gene or 'Per gene' sends directions to give rise to a protein that forms slowly and then splits every 24 hours. The Per gene switches off after generating sufficient PER protein. If the cycle needs 24 hours to finish, it is known as a circadian clock. We disturb the rhythm if we do not take care of ourselves, do not sleep sufficiently, etc.

All Organs have their Respective Clocks

Our bodies do not work on a single clock. Every organ has its own clock, which works for different purposes.

The Most Important Clock : SCN

Our bodies have a master clock that operates in the form of a small group of cells. The set of these cells is known as suprachiasmatic nucleus or SCN. They are situated at the hypothalamus, the center of the brain's base. It encompasses the command hubs for sleep, satiety, hunger, stress response, fluid stability, and so on.

The Three Essential Rhythms

Various organ clocks function like an ensemble to give rise to three primary rhythms that reside at the root of health. These include activity, nutrition and sleep. These rhythms are completely interlinked and we can fully regulate them. When each one of them functions cent percent, it means we have ideal health.

The First Rhythm : Sleep: We Can Control Our Sleep Patterns

People are not morning larks or night owls because of their genes. They fall into these categories because of their habits. Even if a person has a mutation in a gene that causes him or her to sleep less or go to bed too early, he or she can overcome it by changing his or her habits. We can take control of our health.

The Second Rhythm : Food: Our Food Timing Affects Our Clock

The first morning light resets our brain clock. The first bite of the day resets our organ clocks. When we have food can help supersede the master signal from the SCN master clock. Our brain and gut communicate and our gut clock tells the brain when to anticipate breakfast. This is why we feel hungry at the same time every morning. When we eat breakfast at a particular time every day, our brain sends a signal to our stomach to be ready to process the food. This is why we feel hungry at that time every day. If we are traveling and required to wake up and eat earlier than our home time, it changes matters. If we eat breakfast earlier than our regular time on a specific day, we won't feel as hungry as usual before since our brain has not sent the signal to our stomach. If we eat earlier than our usual time, our body will have to stop cleaning and turn off the fat - burning switch since it needs to utilize the fresh food that is coming. Our pancreas, muscles, liver and stomach clocks will also get befuddled.

These clocks will try to expedite but it will be a challenge since they can't be that quick. When we travel, our body creates a new circadian code to adjust to our new surroundings. However, when we come back home, our body will get confused again and our organs will try to adjust by slowing down their work.

The Circadian Clock and Food

With the help of the circadian clock, every single organ is encoded to process food for a number of hours, beginning with breakfast. An 8:00 a. m. breakfast means that our system will carry out its function perfectly for 8 to 10 hours. Every single meal requires the body to digest, absorb, and metabolize, which lasts for a number of hours. The body takes a couple hours to process even a single food bite. When the 10 - hour frame ends, the metabolic organs and the gut will still handle food but their efficiency will drop since they are not supposed to work the entire day. This will make us experience acid reflux or indigestion. A late dinner or snack will mess up our system even more. It will shift our body from fat-burning to fat-making.

When we eat arbitrarily throughout our day and night, the procedure of fat - making will never switch off. The glucose stemming from digested carbohydrates takes over our blood and the liver loses its efficiency to absorb glucose. If we continue to do this for some days, the continuous spike in blood glucose will bring us to a condition of pre-diabetes or diabetes.

If we fail to take our circadian clocks into consideration, keeping track of our calories, working out, steering clear of sweets, carbs and fats and consuming a lot of protein won't help. Timing is extremely significant. We should avoid late dinners. We also need to avoid varying our breakfast timing. The solution is simple. We need to map out an eating schedule and adhere to it.

The Third Rhythm : How Physical Activity Affects Timing

When we are not sleeping or eating, we are supposed to be carrying out some physical activity. According to several studies, physical activity improves sleep in various age groups of people. When sleep becomes better, other outcomes also improve. An improvement in our sleep timing leads to a betterment in our circadian rhythm.

Physical activity refers to any type of movement that leads to energy expenditure. Some examples of physical activity include taking part in sports, shifting weighty objects, carrying out household tasks, gardening, unhurried walking and general exercise.

Chapter 3: Monitor and Test Whether Your Circadian Code is Synchronized

An inconsistent lifestyle or aging causes circadian interruption and a number of diseases. A strict eating schedule, circadian lighting and revitalizing sleep support our circadian rhythm and prevent or reverse such illnesses.

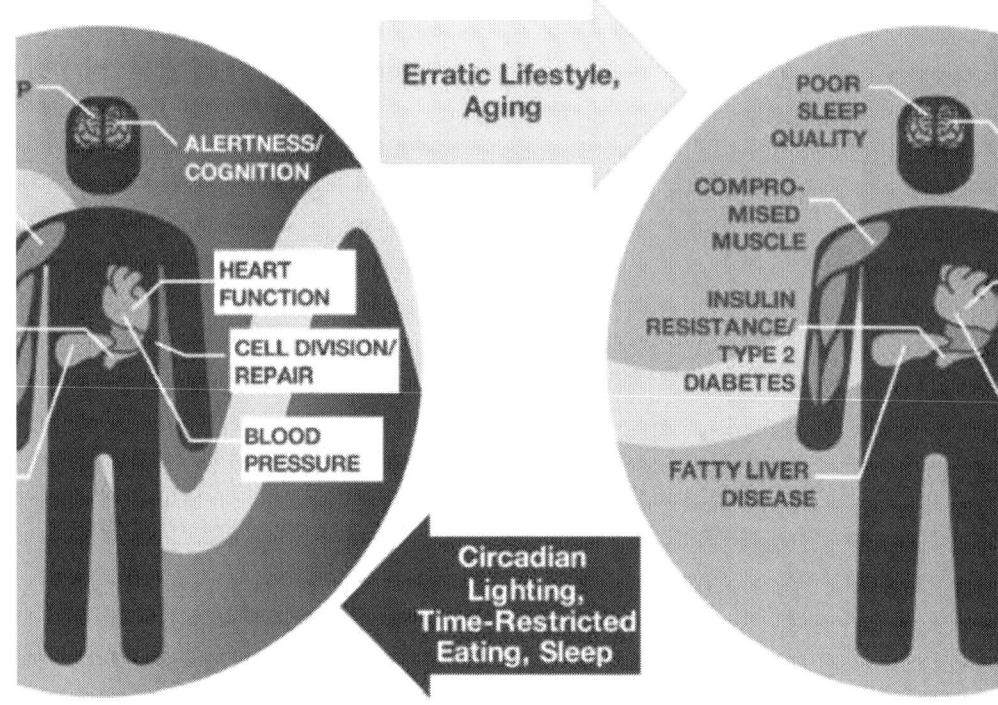

Erratic lifestyle or aging promotes circadian disruption and various diseases. Circadian lighting, time-restricted eating, and restorative sleep sustain our circadian rhythm and prevent or reverse these diseases.

Checking the Strength of your Circadian Code

Quiz: Physical, Mental and Behavioral Segments

PHYSICAL HEALTH

Has your doctor told you that you are overweight?	Y/N
Have you been diagnosed with either prediabetes or diabetes?	Y/N
Are you taking prescription medication for a chronic disease, such as heart disease, blood pressure, cholesterol, asthma, acid reflux, joint pain, or insomnia?	Y/N
Are you taking *over-the-counter* remedies for acid reflux, pain, allergies, or insomnia?	Y/N
Do you have an irregular menstrual cycle?	Y/N
Do you have hot flashes or disrupted sleep related to menopause?	Y/N
Do you have a decreased libido?	Y/N
Have you been diagnosed with a disease linked to chronic inflammation, such as multiple sclerosis or inflammatory bowel disease?	Y/N
Do you have frequent lower back pain?	Y/N
Have you been diagnosed with sleep apnea?	Y/N
Do you snore?	Y/N
Do you wake up feeling congested or with a stuffy nose?	Y/N
Do you have frequent abdominal pain, heartburn, or indigestion?	Y/N
Do you have frequent headaches or migraines?	Y/N
Do your eyes feel tired at the end of the day?	Y/N

MENTAL HEALTH

Do you feel anxious? Y/N

Do you feel low or have frequent blue moods? Y/N

Do you struggle with attention and focus? Y/N

Do you experience brain fog or poor concentration? Y/N

Do you frequently lose items, like your glasses, a charging cable, or keys? Y/N

Are you forgetful of names and faces? Y/N

Do you rely on a calendar or to-do lists? Y/N

Do you get tired in the afternoon? Y/N

Do you wake feeling tired? Y/N

Have you been diagnosed with post-traumatic stress disorder (PTSD)? Y/N

Have you been diagnosed with attention deficit hyperactivity disorder (ADHD), autism spectrum disorder (ASD), or bipolar disorder? Y/N

Do you have food cravings? Y/N

Do you feel like you have a lack of willpower over food? Y/N

Have you been told that you are irritable? Y/N

Do you have trouble making decisions? Y/N

BEHAVIORAL HABITS

Do you take less than 5,000 steps a day?	Y/N
Do you spend less than an hour outdoors under daylight each day?	Y/N
Do you exercise after 9:00 p.m.?	Y/N
Do you spend more than an hour on the computer, your phone, or watching TV before bedtime?	Y/N
Do you have one or more alcoholic drinks (cocktails, wine, or beer) after dinner?	Y/N
Do you forget to drink water throughout the day?	Y/N
Do you drink coffee, tea, or caffeinated soda in the afternoon or evening?	Y/N
Do you consume chocolates, high-carb foods (doughnuts, pizza), or energy drinks to improve your energy level?	Y/N
Do you binge on foods late in the day regardless of hunger?	Y/N
Do you drink or eat anything (other than water) after 7:00 p.m.?	Y/N
Do you sleep with a light on?	Y/N
Do you set aside less than 7 hours for sleep and rest every day?	Y/N
Do you need an alarm clock to wake up in the morning?	Y/N
Do you typically catch up on sleep on the weekends?	Y/N
Do you eat whenever food is presented to you, even if you are not hungry?	Y/N

A majority of us will have some 'yes' answers to these questions since there is certainly some circadian disturbance in our lives. In the physical and mental health segments, having three or more 'yes' answers means that our circadian rhythms might not be working in the best possible manner. Even if others also share your symptoms, it does not mean that it is acceptable. In the behavioral segment, even 'one' yes indicates circadian disturbance. Several people come up with five or more yes responses, which mean that they have room for circadian improvement in several areas.

Tracking Exercise

		What time did you wake up? With or without an alarm clock?	What time did you go to sleep?	What time did you take your first bite/sip of the day?	What time did you take your last bite/sip of the day?	What time did you shut off all screens?	What time did you exercise?
Monday	Time:						
	Alarm?						
Tuesday	Time:						
	Alarm?						
Wednesday	Time:						
	Alarm?						
Thursday	Time:						
	Alarm?						
Friday	Time:						
	Alarm?						
Saturday	Time:						
	Alarm?						
Sunday	Time:						
	Alarm?						

It consists of a chart to fill over a week. We can use it to achieve an ideal circadian rhythm. The author cannot define our ideal code for us. We need to pay attention to our natural rhythms to decide the circadian code that suits us best. We need to make these adjustments to stay healthy in the long run and avoid chronic diseases.

Action Plan

Waking up is the most significant part of the day. We require an alarm clock because our room has been designed to stop natural light from entering it. After sleeping properly, we should be able to wake up ourselves without a clock.

Anything we eat or drink other than water restarts our brain and stomach clock in the morning. Even a cup of coffee or tea counts as a meal.

The last bite of the day needs to become a component of the digestive procedure for 2 - 3 hours before our system can begin its mending and revitalizing. Therefore, we must finish dinner a few hours before bedtime. Culture plays a role in deciding dinner time.

We usually wake up in accord with our work schedule. Bedtime is of essential significance in this context since it plays a role in deciding the amount of sleep we will get.

The time we switch our devices off is significant since our brain takes several minutes after it to wind down.

The timing of exercise holds a significant amount of importance in the context of circadian rhythms and sleep.

The above-mentioned six times will shed light on our current circadian rhythm. The first four classifications are the most significant.

If all six times vary by +/- 2 hours or more over the week, we have a lot of work to do. We need to work on at least one classification in this case. Improving one can improve others at times as well.

How many overall hours do you sleep every night? Adults need at least 7 and children need at least 9 hours of sleep daily. If we are not getting enough sleep, we need to sleep some more. If we still feel sleepy after getting 7 hours of sleep, we need to improve our sleep quality.

If the total time between our first and last bite /sip of the day (excluding water and medication) is more than 12 hours, we need to reduce it. We should consume all our food within 8 to 11 hours to be healthy.

The difference between our last sip/bite time and bedtime should be 3 or more hours. Fixing our timing will fix our health.

Part II: The Circadian Lifestyle

Chapter 4: A Circadian Code to Optimize Sleep

Since we now know the manner in which our circadian code functions, it's time now to master it. Our goal is to modify our activities to the best time during the day and make them accomplish the highest level of harmony with our clocks. We should consume food when our metabolism functions most efficiently. We need to engage in activity when our body and brain are at their zenith. We also need to sleep sufficiently to be able to carry out our tasks the next day. The second part of our goal is to mend disturbances and reorient our clocks to better our health.

Sleep has a number of cycles and stages. Shift workers who have to sleep during daytime do not succeed in getting the required number of sleep cycles.

Adults should give themselves a chance of 8 sequential sleep hours and children 10. This includes going to bed, achieving a comfortable position, and going to sleep. The actual sleep time for adults should be at least 7 hours and for children, 9 hours.

Sleep debt is the difference between our required quantity of sleep and the actual sleep we get. If we stay awake for 2 days, we will feel like sleeping for a long time because of our sleep debt but our circadian clock will not let us sleep for 16 straight hours. This will give rise to a clash until we catch up.

Napping will help us pay some of our sleep debt. However, we should avoid a long afternoon nap since it will stop us from going to bed early at night.

Sleep and Life Span : The U Curve

Research indicates that those who sleep a lot less than the necessary 7 hours have more probability to experience an early death. Those who sleep for 10 to 11 hours daily are also likely to have a small life span. Too much and too little sleep are both bad.

Two-Phase Sleep

Contrary to myth, people in ancient times did not sleep in two phases. They got continuous sleep in one go. Two - phase sleep is more a pattern of our modern lifestyle. A lot of people wake up after sleeping for 3 to 4 hours. They cannot sleep after waking up this way and either read, eat or use the computer.

Is Your Sleep Quality Sufficient?

To judge whether you sleep well or not, ask the following questions:

1: At what time do you go to bed and how much time do you take before falling asleep?

Insomnia stems from worry/stress, excessive food, lack of sufficient physical activity, and spending excessive time in bright light in the evening. We should note that if we spend a lot of time outdoors, it helps us bear with nighttime indoor light more easily.

2: What's the number of times you wake up during sleep?

When we wake up more than once during sleep for at least some minutes and it's not easy to get back to sleep, it is known as fragmented sleep. When we sleep this way, our brain will record less sleep than we actually get. Fragmented sleep becomes more probable with age. We can avoid fragmented sleep by synchronizing our sleep time and circadian code.

Fragmented sleep occurs because of snoring, sleep apnea, noise, dehydration, acid reflux (because of eating too late), ambient temperature that is excessively cold or hot, or sleeping next to a pet.

3: After waking up in the morning, do you feel sufficiently rested?

If you feel sleepy or foggy after waking up or if you need an alarm to wake up, then you are not properly rested and need more sleep.

Insufficient Sleep Disturbs our Circadian Code

Sleep - deprivation leaves a negative effect on our outcomes and functions all around. It leads to a decline in performance, brain fog, and unclear thinking. This leaves a negative effect on our attention, response time and decisions. In small children, insufficient sleep can cause irritability and a tendency to act challenging. A repeated lack of sleep can give rise to severe consequences. Research indicates that children who have attention deficit hyperactivity disorder (ADHD) show less symptoms when they have slept sufficiently at night and have had natural light exposure during the day. Sleep-deprived adults become prone to depression and anxiety and the elderly might face a weak memory.

When we do not sleep sufficiently, we dedicate that time to something else like eating more or staying more in light at night. A lack of sleep also leaves an effect on our satiety and hunger hormones. Sleep deprivation causes us to engage in excessive eating.

Chronic Sleep Issue Indicators

One of the signs of a lack of sleep is joint pain. Too much light at night will cause us to eat more and lead to poor sleep. Having late - night snacks will affect our functioning. It is better for our brain to have a long fasting period.

Action Plan

Daytime Habits that can Improve Sleep

Wake up early if you wish to go to sleep early.

Physical activity, especially outdoor activity under daylight, will boost the drive to sleep.

Lessen your caffeine intake after the middle of the day to sleep more easily.

Meals, Sleep and Timing

Avoid eating late since it leaves a negative effect on both sleep and metabolism. A time-restricted eating (TRE) routine of 8-9 hours can improve sleep. Avoiding alcohol will also help us sleep better.

Avoid late-night snacks to stop your acid reflux problem, which might wake you in the middle of the night. If you wake up in the middle of the night, avoid eating.

Darkness is Essential for Sleep

Keep your sleeping environment dark. Avoid exposure to light during the evening as much as possible. If you want, use an eye mask for sleeping.

Give teens an early dinner and teach them not to stay in bright light in the evening.

Small lightning changes will go a long way. Dim lights/switches also help.

Tips to Improve Sleep

Sufficient sleep leads to better performance and concentration the next day. If you cannot sleep properly, try the following :

Bring down the temperature in your bedroom to 70 degree Fahrenheit or lesser. If you cannot control the temperature, take a warm bath or shower before going to sleep. Pay attention to your blankets if you wake up feeling too hot. Avoid foam mattresses.

To avoid the sounds and sirens outside, triple - pane window glass, a fan, a white - noise machine or a white - noise app can all help.

If sound calms you down, you can listen to relaxing music on a timer on your smartphone or radio to go to sleep.

Use earplugs if you are an extremely light sleeper.

Age does not matter. We can easily sleep at any age by using these techniques.

Pointers to Stop Snoring

Snoring can really affect sleep. Some methods that can help avoid snoring include a neti pot or a saline spray. A sleeping aid can also help keep the nose open. If these techniques do not help, consult an ENT specialist or a pulmonary medicine sleep specialist.

The Problem with Sleep Apnea

Obstructive sleep apnea (OSA) can give rise to sleep deprivation as well. Some but not all with this condition snore. It also leaves a negative effect on brain health. It serves as a risk factor for heart disease and stroke. A sleep study can help find out if a person has sleep apnea. Medical professionals prescribe a device called continuous positive airway pressure (CPAP) for sleep apnea.

Sleep Medications

Some people have to use sleep medications to go to sleep. However, this is not a permanent solution to sleep issues. The author recommends that the people who think they need sleep meds to sleep should try a top quality melatonin supplement first.

Tackling Sleep the Behavioral Way

Don't pay attention to your phone/clock/watch when you can't sleep. Avoid these devices to avoid their light.

Do not be concerned about bedtime or waking up late the next morning. Use an alarm clock till you are synchronized with your circadian code. Utilize deep belly breathing to relax.

Do not be concerned about the previous night. You will not repeat a bad episode.

Do not be concerned about how many hours of sleep you are getting. You might require less sleep than others. However, if you are not feeling fresh, try the tips shared earlier.

How to Wake Up the Best Possible Way

To wake up fresh, sleep sufficiently by going to sleep early.

Come face to face with bright light right after waking up.

Engage in a quick morning walk (5 to 15 minutes). Leave your home and engage in some activity to come face to face with bright daylight.

Try to wake up at the same time every single day. Waking up later on the weekends (2 hours or more) indicates a lack of restorative sleep during the week.

Chapter 5: Time-restricted Eating: Preparing Your Clock for Weight Loss

The entirety of nutrition science revolves around two ideas: limiting calories and having a healthy diet. However, modern experiments conducted on mice and humans have demonstrated that regardless of what we eat, the timing of food is everything. When we avoid eating late at night and restrict eating to 8 or a few more hours the whole day, we lose weight. Food timing is more important than food type.

Don't Eat Like a Shift Worker

A study found that when overweight people who first ate within a 14-hour plus window started eating within an identical 10-hour window daily, they lost a substantial amount of weight. Their sleep at night and energy levels during the day improved. Their hunger levels also declined.

Therefore, we should synchronize our eating schedule with our circadian code.

Action Plan

Mapping Out a TRE Day

Begin by underlining your breakfast timing, whether it's a bite or your first cup of tea/ coffee. It starts the eating window. If breakfast starts at 8 a. m., dinner should end by 8 p. m. The earlier the breakfast, the better. It will also mean having dinner as early as possible

Night fasting is critically significant during the last couple of hours. It cleans our system. We should not have breakfast earlier than usual if we are on a 12-hour eating cycle. If we are following an eating window of 8 to 10 hours, we can have an early breakfast once in a while.

We can eat any type of food within our eating window but we should adhere to consistent meal times. Brushing our teeth will not disturb our schedule.

It is completely okay to feel hungry in the morning. Eat more. Give importance to protein and fiber. A proper breakfast will keep you full for hours.

The best kind of breakfast is balanced. It includes complex carbohydrates or fiber, nourishing fats and lean protein. Fiber - rich foods help regulate blood sugar the whole day. Eating protein early initiates stomach acid secretion. Replace most of your dinner protein intake with breakfast protein intake. It will help you avoid unhealthy snacking. It will also keep you full for 4 to 6 hours. You can have a salad or soup for lunch to avoid the lethargy that stems from a heavy meal.

Breakfast and dinner are the most significant meals to synchronize with our circadian rhythms since they mark the start and end of our eating cycle.

Followers of TRE do not feel as hungry as before at dinnertime. They eventually end up eating less for dinner. Dinner can be a combination of protein, vegetables and healthy fats. We should avoid simple carbs at dinnertime. A time difference of 3 to

4 hours between the last bite and bedtime leads to improved digestion and sleep.

We will stop feeling hungry after our set dinnertime once we start following TRE. If we have a late snack, it will just stay in our stomach since it's closed. This is called a food hangover.

How to Approach Dinner Drinking

If you want to have a drink at dinner, have it either before dinner or along with it. Don't take it after dinner.

Hydrate properly. Hydration plays a role in our circadian rhythm. We should have a glass of water every one or two hours. We can have water after dinner or even when we wake up in the middle of the night. Coffee and tea after dinner are not acceptable. Decaffeinated herbal teas without any sweeteners can act like water intake and are acceptable.

Daytime versus Nighttime Snacking

Daytime snacks are acceptable but nighttime snacks are not. You must stick to healthy options. An occasional birthday cake or cookie is okay. Avoid late night snacks even if you feel hungry in the initial days of following TRE. Have water if you feel hungry in the middle of the night. Late - night hunger will go away after some time. Stomach cramping also results from late-night eating.

Stick to your schedule on weekends as well.

Important Answers

12-hour TRE is for everyone from children aged 5 and older to teens to adults with different health issues.

We can choose any 12 hours for TRE but starting as early as possible is the best choice.

Since TRE is a lifestyle instead of a diet, we can combine it with any diet including ketogenic, Atkins, Paleo, and so on

We can even use TRE and periodic fasting, such as a 5:2 diet. In this case, we will use TRE during the five days we eat.

If you feel dizzy because of following TRE, stop following it and consult your physician. Also, if you change abruptly from a 16-hour eating window to an 8-hour one, it might not suit you. First change to a 12-hour window and then improve your diet gradually.

This program has a 6-week impediment since its benefits usually start unfolding after 6 weeks. Be patient and do not lose hope.

Medications do not come into the category of food. Take them as prescribed.

Avoid coffee after 12 pm. If you are a shift worker and take coffee before driving home in the morning to sleep, avoid it since it will create sleep issues. Use carpooling or public transportation in such cases.

TRE is something you can stick to all your life. 8 hours might not work forever but 10 to 12 hours can.

You can have a cheat day at times.

You can use this chart to track your progress

Month one	First bite	Last bite	Hours slept	Noticeable changes in health, mood, or energy
Day 1				
2				
3				
4				
5				
6				
7				
8				
9				
10				
11				
12				
13				
14				
15				
16				
17				
18				
19				
20				
21				
22				
23				
24				
25				
26				
27				
28				
29				
30				
31				

Foods to Avoid for TRE

Avoid 7 types of foods including soda (diet or others), prepackaged vegetable and fruit juices, breakfast cereals, energy protein and fruit-and-nut bars, processed foods that have fructose, sucrose or corn syrup, hot or dark chocolate in the evening and commercially processed nut butter. Only use peanut butter that has nuts. Avoid the ones with added oil or sugar.

If you are a vegetarian, use better proteins such as cottage cheese or tofu. Lentils only have a limited amount of protein.

Proteins are Essential

Humans, animals and plants need proteins since they contain crucial amino acids. Capitalize on different sources of protein. Foods with high protein content include animal meat, poultry, seafood, fish, peas and beans, seeds, nuts, soy, eggs, etc. Dairy and leafy green vegetables also have protein. The best protein sources are animal proteins.

Too much protein can harm your body. The recommended intake is 0.36 grams of protein per body weight pound daily. If you want a protein drink, choose one that does not have added sugar.

Go for Complex Carbohydrates

Best carbohydrates are nonstarchy ones. Some of the best sources include leafy green vegetables and fruits and grains with a low glycemic index (GI).

Restrict or avoid simple carbohydrates such as pasta, white rice, white bread, cakes, cookies and pastries. Go for whole wheat counterparts since they have high fiber content. Our body cannot digest fiber and fiber detoxifies it. Good choices include quinoa, beans, whole grains, berries and leafy green vegetables.

Good alternatives to white rice and basmati rice include brown rice and parboiled rice.

Best Healthy Fat Sources

Dietary fat is extremely significant for our body as well. Some healthy sources include butter, egg yolks, seeds, nuts, avocados and olive oil. Butter falls into the saturated fat category. The rest is monounsaturated fatty acids.

Omega - 3 and omega - 6 fats are polyunsaturated fats. They are also good for health. Good sources of omega-3 fats include flax, some eggs and some fish including shrimp and salmon.

Omega-6 sources include safflower, soybean and corn oil. Pork, beef and chicken also contain polyunsaturated fats.

Shopping List for the Circadian Code

Low-Glycemic Fruits and Vegetables

Apples	Beet greens	Cabbage	Parsnips	Cauliflower	Fiddleheads	Kiwis	Squash
Apricots	Bell peppers	Carrots	Peaches	Celery	Figs	Leeks	Strawberries
Artichokes	Blackberries	Melons	Pears	Coconuts	Garlic	Raspberries	Swiss chard
Arugula	Blueberries	Mushrooms	Peppers	Collard greens	Grapefruit	Romaine lettuce	Tomatoes
Asparagus	Bok choy	Mustard greens	Prunes	Cucumbers	Jerusalem artichokes	Rutabaga	Turnip greens
Avocados	Broccoli	Olives	Pumpkin	Eggplant	Jicama	Sea vegetables	Watercress
Bananas	Brussels sprouts	Onions	Radishes	Fennel	Kale	Spinach	

Protein from Animal Sources

| Beef | Chicken | Eggs | Pork | Veal |
| Bison/Buffalo | Duck | Lamb | Turkey | |

Vegetarian Proteins

| Black beans | Garbanzo beans (chickpeas) | Legumes | Navy beans | Pinto beans | Sugar snap peas |
| Black-eyed peas | Kidney beans | Lentils | Peanuts | Split peas | White beans |

Fish and Shellfish

Catfish	Crab	Haddock	Lobster	Octopus	Salmon	Shrimp	Swordfish
Clams	Crayfish	Halibut	Mackerel	Oysters	Scallops	Snapper	Trout
Cod	Flounder	Herring	Mussels	Pollock	Sea bass	Squid (calamari)	Tuna

Nuts

| Almonds | Chestnuts | Macadamia nuts | Pine nuts | Walnuts |
| Brazil nuts | Hazelnuts | Pecans | Pistachios | Derivative nut butters |

Seeds

Chia seeds   Pumpkin seeds

Flaxseeds   Sesame seeds

Hemp seeds   Sunflower seeds

Healthy Fats and Oils

Avocado oil   Macadamia oil

Butter   Olive oil

Coconut oil

Chapter 6: The Best Way to Learn and Work

Every single thing we do needs learning. Every task requires work by both the brain and the body. Our brain function is at its peak between 10 a. m. and 3 p. m. This is the best time for learning and work. This is the time frame during which our mind is best equipped to make good decisions, solve multidimensional issues, and handle complex social situations. As we reach our day's end, our brain gets tired and we cannot carry out complex tasks. If we have a heavy lunch, we feel sleepy. Starting at 3 p.m., our mood and attention deteriorate. It is best to optimize our morning and get most of our work done early, during our most functional hours. A lack of proper sleep the previous night can worsen the situation.

Action Plan

Don't try to wake yourself up with sugar. Have water or hot decaffeinated tea. You can also have nuts or some fruit. Water is still your best option.

You might like to work at night but your brain cannot be at its best at night.

Tips

Staying awake more hours will not add to your productivity. Dedicate 8 hours of sleep opportunity to be prepared tomorrow.

Use natural light during daytime to maximize your productivity and alertness.

Handle light in the evening to be ready for restorative sleep.

Use Light to Add to Your Productivity

Maximize light during the day and minimize it, especially from the blue spectrum, during the night.

The Link between Food and Productivity

To give rise to a powerful circadian rhythm, eat at identical times daily. Stick to this especially when it comes to breakfast and dinner. As far as what we eat between these two meals is concerned, we should focus on quality. We need to eat foods that support healthy brain function.

Coffee

Coffee might boost our alertness but it only postpones our sleep debt.

Sleep is essential since sleep deprivation disturbs our circadian code for learning.

School start times should be pushed later since children and teens need their sleep. They also need to avoid light as much as possible in the evening.

Smartboards are not ideal since they are used in dark rooms. Bright classrooms and offices are better.

Chapter 7: Align Your Exercise with your Circadian Code

Action Plan

Exercise is extremely significant in our lives and in relation to the circadian code. According to the American Heart Association (AHA), healthy people need 150 minutes of moderate exercise or 75 minutes of enthusiastic exercise weekly. They can also choose a blend of both. Exercise can be any physical activity that includes body movement and calorie burning. Some types of exercise include aerobic exercise, strength or resistance training, and stretching exercises.

Walking is beneficial all around. Exercise improves sleep and the circadian rhythm.

Exercise Timing

If you can't exercise in one go for 30 to 45 minutes, split your time into three 10 to 15 minute sessions. When we combine exercise with TRE, it becomes all the more likely that we will burn fat.

Early morning Exercise

Early morning exercise is great. Its benefits are several. Daylight exposure will align our brain clock. It will add to our alertness and lessen depression. If it is cold, we will trigger brown fat and boost the likelihood of fat burning. It will raise our cortisol level in the morning and lessen inflammation.

Late Afternoon Exercise

Between 3 p. m. and dinnertime is also a great time for exercise.

Exercise After Dinner

If you cannot manage to exercise at the above - mentioned two times, you can exercise after dinner since it is better than nothing.

Night-Shift Workers and Exercise

Night-shift workers need exercise too. Exercise can reset the circadian clocks all over our brain and body. Night - shift workers can exercise at night since it will help them curb sleep as well.

TRE Leaves a Positive Effect on Exercise Performance

The three advantages include better muscle mass, boosted endurance exercise capacity and improved motor coordination in mice. This applies to humans too.

Chapter 8: Handling the Core Causes of "Disruption": Screens and Light

Modern light took us away from natural light almost a century ago. However, the real circadian collapse has originated from the rise of digital screens. We are surrounded by news and entertainment for 24 hours. It never stops. However, light, even if it is dim, disturbs our circadian rhythm.

Action Plan

Firstly, we need to lessen blue light from screens since it will limit evening light exposure. We can buy televisions with this technology or use add-ons to save money. An example is Drift TV.

How to Fix Home Lighting

Even though LED lights are energy-efficient, they have more blue light, which hinders sleep. New tunable LED lights are being developed. These alter color and dim as well. We can switch to semi-natural lighting by amplifying blue light for daytime and amber-colored light for nighttime. This will replicate the natural day - night cycle. These tunable lights will be costly for now.

Another current solution is to add dimmer switches to LED lights. These switches can provide bright light during the day and dim light at night. We can install different kinds of lights in different rooms as well.

For night bathroom visits, we can also use motion - triggered path lighting that illuminates the floor.

We can also use amber - colored bulbs with a tinge of orange. They don't have too much blue light and won't disturb our circadian clock a lot.

When we need light in the evening for homework or reading, we should use table lamps.

Since red lights have the least blue light, changing night lights in children's bedrooms to red light can increase their sleep duration.

Light and Teenagers

Teenage boys like darkness. We should encourage them to let natural light in during the day and set their phone and computer screens to release less blue light 2 hours before bedtime.

Blue - light Filtering Eye Glasses

These glasses also help at home and outside.

You Might Not Need Sunglasses

Unless you are going to the beach or on a road trip, you can avoid sunglasses. You need daylight if you spend most of your time indoors. Avoid looking directly at the sun.

Part III: How to Enhance Circadian Health

Chapter 9: The Clock, Digestive Issues and the Microbiome

Digestive issues and concerns are quite common these days. The digestive process consists of stages and every single stage has a circadian constituent, from ingestion to elimination. A leaky gut indicates a severe issue.

Different foods are digested in different ways. There is definitely a clock in the gut. Furthermore, gut function leaves a significant impact on overall health.

The Circadian Nature of the Gut Microbiome

Gut microbiome composition alters between day and night. When we go to sleep at night, the set of bacteria in our stomach is different from the one we will wake up with and the one emerging midday. Every bacteria category digests different kinds of nutrients. To sustain a diverse gut microbiome, we should eat the kind of food that is full of miscellaneous nutrition sources. Experiments on rodents indicate that TRE boosts the gut microbiome so that the gut successfully and effectively handles and absorbs nutrients and eliminates waste. This improves health.

What we eat and the gut microbiome join forces to generate a number of hormones and chemicals that leave an effect on our mood and can play a role in the feelings of calmness, panic, mania, depression or anxiety. Gut microbiome is also linked with autism. We should choose foods that shield our gut microbiome. Circadian disturbances give rise to digestive illnesses. Also, those who take acid medications for months are doing it wrong since it can lead to disadvantages.

Irritable bowel syndrome (IBS) is a gastrointestinal disorder and its signs and symptoms include gas, bloating, cramping, changed bowel habits and abdominal pain. TRE also make matters better in this regard and assists IBS patients.

Chapter 10: The Circadian Code Helps with Metabolic Syndrome : Heart Disease, Obesity and Diabetes

When our body's metabolism does not work properly anymore, it leaves an effect on the digestion of sugar ,fat and cholesterol. This leads to weight gain, which causes metabolic diseases such as heart disease, obesity and diabetes. They can emerge separately or together but one's symptoms can precede others'. With a buildup of these illnesses and their symptoms, the regular function of the remainder of the body suffers, which is known as 'metabolic syndrome.' Metabolic syndrome is known as the existence of any three of five characteristics including high blood pressure, abdominal obesity, fasting hyperglycemia, high-density lipoprotein -cholesterol (HDL-C) levels and laboratory abnormalities of triglycerides (a fat type in the blood). Metabolic syndrome is deadly but fully reversible.

Action Plan

The solution to prevent and reverse this syndrome includes adapting to a healthier circadian code, exercise and weight loss.

Some of us have a night eating syndrome. TRE can help with it but if we really want to eat at night, we can try a late TRE, with our first meal starting around lunchtime. An issue with circadian rhythms is linked to obesity and type II diabetes. Circadian rhythm disruption can lead to heart disease as well. TRE assists with all these issues by improving our body's systems and functions. It further boosts the efficiency of metabolic syndrome medications.

Chapter 11: To Boost the Immune System and Treat Cancer

The immune system has a circadian element as well. If we resync it successfully, we can control how it works. The circadian code is the solution to several of today's problems. Mastering our code can speed up recovery. Our medications for different diseases should work in synchronization with circadian scheduling. TRE assists with inflammation as well.

As stated earlier, shift work with circadian disruption has officially been declared aa a carcinogen. Cancer has a variety of causes and some of them have a circadian a possible carcinogenic component. Therefore, circadian rhythm is significant in the context of both cancer prevention and its treatment. Research also supports the idea that a strong circadian rhythm can shield from cancer.

Chapter 12: The Circadian Code for Improving Brain Health

Indoor lighting at the wrong moment can leave a negative effect on our circadian code. Premature babies kept in the NICU experience too much light. Research indicates that covering their cribs at night for a few hours improved several health outcomes for them. We can fight depression with the correct kind of light as well.

Light and sleep play an extremely significant role in the context of brain health. Sleep disruption is the root of neurological diseases. Too much exposure to light at night is bad. TRE supports better brain function as well since it will lead to the body generating ketones, which will foster the brain and lessen brain inflammation. Exercise improves brain health as well.

Chapter 13: The Best Kind of Circadian Day

When we stay on schedule and finish the whole day's eating from breakfast to dinner within 8 to 12 hours and include exercise in this time frame, it translates into the best kind of circadian day. All of us will have days where we cannot stick to a perfect schedule. It is acceptable. If you have a late dinner one night, try to delay your breakfast the next day. We should adjust ourselves and still stick to TRE despite some glitches here and there.

Conclusion

In brief, even though we might not be in the best of health right now, the solution to our health problems is simple: we need to rectify our timing. When we change our waking, eating and sleeping timings and bring these in harmony with our circadian rhythms, it will make our life better in all areas. Following the action plan in this summary is simple but can lead to wonders. Let us all improve our lives by respecting Father Time.

Check out other summaries

1- Summary of **GIRL, WASH YOUR FACE** - Stop Believing the Lies About Who You Are so You Can Become Who You Were Meant to Be: Key Takeaways & Analysis from **Rachel Hollis**'s book

https://www.amazon.com/dp/B07NPP6Y2T

2- Summary of **The Life-Changing Magic of Tidying Up** - The Japanese Art of Decluttering and Organizing: Key Takeaways & Analysis from **Marie Kondō**'s book

https://www.amazon.com/dp/B07P1NF4T7

3- Summary of **Medical Medium Liver Rescue** - Key Takeaways & Analysis from **Anthony William**'s book

https://www.amazon.com/dp/B07PT3X67P

4- Summary of **EXTREME OWNERSHIP** - How U.S. Navy SEALs Lead and Win: Key Takeaways & Analysis from **Jocko Willink and Leif Babin**'s book

https://www.amazon.com/dp/B07NL4QZDY

5- Summary of **Educated- A Memoir** - Key Takeaways & Analysis from **Tara Westover**'s book

https://www.amazon.com/dp/B07P8LBM3P

6- Summary of **The Circadian Code by Dr. Satchin Panda** - Lose Weight, Supercharge Your Energy, and Transform Your Health from Morning to Midnight

https://www.amazon.com/dp/B07PV16L1L

Made in the USA
Coppell, TX
19 July 2020